Tico's Book

By Lunatico Conure
Illustrated By
Carol Atkinson Durr

For our children's children

Milan Galvis
Antonia Durr
&
Tate Galvis

 Bay Media, Inc.

Published by Bay Media, Inc.
550M Ritchie Highway, #271
Severna Park, MD 21146
(410) 647-8402 - Fax (410) 544-4640
Web site: http://www.baymed.com

I was scared that day in October when I flew from Texas to Baltimore. I was too young to be flying alone.

My half moon conure grandparents, who lived in Central America, were accustomed to flying long distances. They lived in termite mounds and had to search in vines and on bushes for food. But I, and two other half moon conures, hatched at the Rockport Roost bird nursery near Corpus Christi. We never had to hunt for food or water.

Miss Elke took good care of me at the Roost and even fed me by hand. When I was eight weeks old and ready to fly, she put me in a carrier where I had food, water and a perch to sit on. I flew on a big airplane.

I still wear a purple metal band on my left leg. The letters and numbers are a secret code for where I was hatched. That way if I get lost, someone could help me get back home. My band reads "RRTX 391." That means that I was bird #391 hatched at the Rockport Roost in Texas.

But even with Miss Elke's preparations and my ID bracelet, I was frightened. I had never been in a carrier. Or in a car. Or on an airplane.

Everything made me afraid.

When I arrived at the Baltimore airport, I was still scared. I didn't know the people who came to get me. They were Tia Tica and Bill, but they were strangers when they took me to their car. We took a long drive, me still in my carrier. Finally, when we got to my new home, Tia Tica was so happy to have me she said, "Hello, Tico," and reached her hand in to bring me out.

I bit her.

It was a good bite.

Tia Tica bled.

The first few days I just sat around feeling sad.

Now my home is a big green metal cage with lots of perches, a ladder, a couple of food dishes and a water bottle. The top opens up so I can sit on the roof and look around. Tia Tica gave me some balls, bells and other things to play with.

Some people say that half moon conures are little birds with a big attitude. I'm not sure what that means. Does that mean

I like to be the boss?

I'm sorry to report that I can't fly well. Whenever my wing feathers begin to grow enough for me to soar, Tia Tica and Bill bring out the scissors and clip a few wing feathers. It doesn't hurt. It's like having a hair cut. But I don't like it. I squawk and carry on whenever I see the scissors coming.

One day when I saw the scissors coming, I jumped down from my perch and ran. I hid under the bed, next to the baseball bat, for a long time.

I'm a good bird. I don't wake up too early and scream and holler like some birds. Each night when I go to bed, Tia Tica puts a big colorful towel over my cage, and that makes me feel warm and cozy. I go to the top of my cage on my wavy perch and snuggle down for the night. In the morning I'm quiet until Tia Tica comes to my cage and takes off the cover. Tia Tica says, "Good Morning," then we chuckle and talk, and I get on her hand so we can go to my little stand in the dining room. There Tia Tica tells me, "Poop, poop." I make a direct hit on the paper below.

She's proud of me.   And I'm proud, too.

Actually, I'm good about not messing up on someone's shoulder or shirt. Early on I learned where I should go "poop, poop." Sometimes I'll even say "be-beep" to let everyone know I should be taken to my cage or perch.

But don't look behind the sofa. I'd lose my good reputation for being house trained.

When I get up in the morning, I always go with Tia Tica into the bathroom, where she brushes her teeth and I play with a ball and rattle the glass next to the sink. I screech and cluck when I grab the water glass and shake it.

I've tossed two glasses onto the tile floor.

They broke!

My ball is for a cat, but because it has holes, I can grab it with either my foot or my beak and throw it. Often it goes into the sink, but sometimes it bounces around on the floor. Like a soccer player I'm pretty good at stopping a rolling ball. But I can't kick.

One morning when we
were in the bathroom, Tia
Tica put me on the towel bar
to wait for her. She flushed
the toilet, then put me back
on her shoulder. While I
was clinging to her
shoulder, Tia Tica reached
down to pick up the trash can
for emptying. I was young then
and couldn't hold on well.
I slid off her shoulder and fell into the flushing toilet.

I can't swim.

But Tia Tica was very quick. I was saved.

After we leave the bathroom and Tia Tica's getting dressed, I find Bill. He's still asleep, but I walk up his blanket-covered body and get to his head so that I can peck at his neck and nose. If I'm gentle, he doesn't seem to mind.

But sometimes I find an especially interesting spot on his chin, and I nibble too hard.

Then Bill rolls over and tells me to go away.

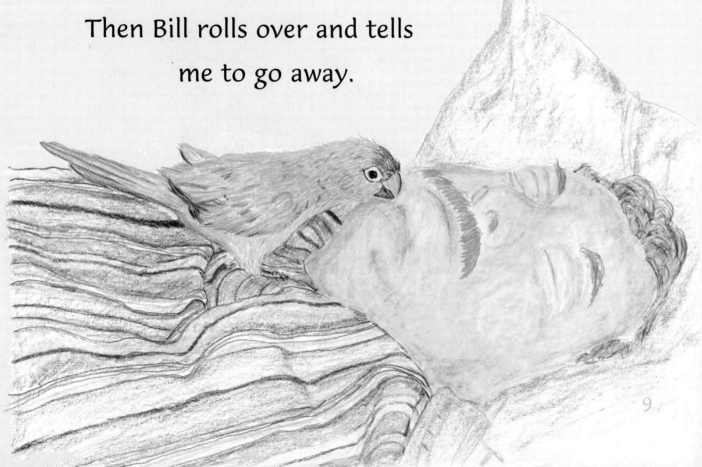

Bill is my favorite. He doesn't make me do things. I like to drink the milk in his cereal bowl and sit on his shoulder while he does the crossword puzzle.

I must be strong, because one morning at breakfast I tilted Bill's cereal bowl and spilled the milk all over the table and floor.

That day
I wasn't
Bill's favorite!

I spilled the cereal only once. Most of the time at breakfast I nibble on cereal or gnaw on his shirt. Many of his shirts have Tico holes. Bill and Tia Tica often have crumbs on their shoulders.

10

Some mornings after breakfast I have a shower. Tia Tica puts my perch in the kitchen sink, and I sit on the branch, ready to get wet. I fluff up my feathers and get all excited. Tia gets the spray bottle and squirts me. I raise my wings and flap a lot and get really soaked.

When I'm wet, I don't look much like a bird. My feathers stick together, and I look skinny. But it doesn't take long for me to dry off and be handsome again.

Soon after moving to Maryland I learned to say "Bill."

One of my most frequent expressions is, "Where's Bill?" I say that when I see him. Then I say "See Bill." I have good ears, so when I hear Bill's car in the carport, I start saying, "Where's Bill?" Then when he comes into the house, I say, "See Bill."

From my cage I also watch across our little bridge so I can see Bill coming back to the house. Then I always say,

"Where's Bill?"
"See Bill."

Then Bill comes in, and I'm pleased with my announcement.

Once when Bill and I were spending the weekend alone together, we were sitting out on the deck. I got rather bold and bit him on the ear. His response was a swift swat. I jumped and tried to fly away, but I bumped into the window.

I fell to the deck and lay there with my feet up in the air. Then Bill got panicky and picked me up, telling me, "Don't you die!" Bill knew he might be in a lot of trouble if Tia Tica came home and discovered

I was dead.

Fortunately after a few minutes I began to wake up. But I didn't have much to say for the whole next day. Days later when Tia Tica came home, I was back to normal. I didn't tell her about this - but Bill did.

While I was still young, I started learning tricks. Tia Tica taught me how to shake hands. She says "Shake," and I lift my right foot and hold her finger. Then Tia Tica says,

"How do you do?"

I think,

"I do just fine."

Actually I'm "left footed" and almost always use my left foot to grab and hold things.

But I learned that to shake hands, you use the right foot.
So I do.

14

I've also learned to "be an eagle." When someone tells me to "be an eagle," I stand up as tall as I can and raise both wings.

I even screech!

Something else I've learned is banking. Tia Tica has a baby shoe bank just my size, and she puts coins on the table near it. When Tia Tica tells me "Go to the bank," I pick up a coin and drop it in the slot.

It was hard learning how to make the coin fall in. At first I had to twist and turn the coin to make it fit in the slot. But I'm good at that now.

Sometimes I fool them. Instead of going to the bank, I drop the coin in their coffee or juice.

"Pretty good," by the way, is some-thing I like to say. I say it sometimes when I'm sipping orange juice out of Tia's glass. But other times I just say "Es bueno."

Tia Tica knows what I mean.

Other things that I can say are:
"What cha doing?"
"Tico talks." (I can't say "s" so it's really "Tico talk".)
"Thank you."   (I'm very polite.)
"Look at you!"

Often Tia Tica tells me, "You be a good bird," so I've learned to say that as well.

I like orange juice and other good things - like cereal, nuts and pretzels. I really like eggs and grits. That's especially good for breakfast. When I'm at the table, I enjoy grabbing juice glasses and shaking them, just like in the bathroom.

But I also like to rattle the spoon in the cereal bowl. It makes a lot of noise! I enjoy that.

There are two things I should NEVER eat - avocados and chocolate. I bet they are both REALLY good.

But I've never had them because they would make me very sick.

My favorite food is cookies. Bill and I love Tahoe cookies. When I hear Bill in the kitchen opening the cookie drawer, I get excited.   When I hear the cookie bag being opened, I go crazy!   My eyes get all jittery, go big and little. I squawk and shriek until Bill shares.

Most of the time I'll say **"Thank you"** to him.

But not always...

Yes, Tahoe cookies do have chocolate.   But Bill never gives me the part with chocolate. He eats all the chocolate himself - just for me!

Another favorite food is BUTTER. I love
butter. And whenever I see it on the counter,
I rush over to eat it.

Yum, yum.

Next to my cage in the living room is a weather alert radio. Tia Tica and Bill need it to know when there is going to be a bad storm.

Each Wednesday there is a test to find out if the weather radio is working okay.

The loud buzzer on it makes a lot of noise. Since the noise is so close and loud, I begin to screech and scream back. I act like a wild and crazy bird, standing up really tall with my beak wide open. I can't stand that weather radio! I may have to learn how to turn it off myself. Maybe Tia Tica will help me.

I often go outside on Tia Tica's shoulder. Because my wings are clipped, I can't fly away. But there are lots of dangers outside for a little bird. When something startles me, I jump and flutter to the ground. If another animal is around, I could become an afternoon snack!

I help in the garden when Tia Tica pulls weeds. I might stay on her shoulder or hang onto her shirt.

Or maybe Tia Tica will put me on a tree branch so I can watch.

Tia Tica really would like me to be on her shoulder

when she walks in the neighborhood each morning. She

even bought me a little purple harness so that I'd be safe

and not flap away. But the first time Tia Tica put it on

me, I fell over on my back

and refused to move.

I just lay there with my feet in the air.

She never tried that again.

That doesn't keep me from going places though. Tia Tica likes to take me on car trips to visit family and friends. I have lots of cages for these occasions. One is quite small and will fit into a canvas bag. One day I went with her and her friends to a barbecue restaurant in North Carolina for lunch. I was in the little cage in the canvas bag.

I was very good and only chirped and chortled softly while they ate barbecue. But as we were leaving the restaurant, I couldn't help letting my presence be known and gave a really big wolf whistle. Everyone looked around - but they didn't see me,

because I was in the canvas bag.

A lot of time during the year I'm molting. That means that my new feathers are coming in and my old ones are falling out. I spend a lot of time preening - pecking at the new feathers that are in little cases and making the cases fall off. It makes a mess on Tia Tica's and Bill's shoulders, but I'm a clean bird and want to make myself look my best.

When I'm molting, it's hard for me to get to the new feathers coming out on my head. I can't reach them with my beak. I look like I have lots of little horns growing on my head. I'm glad when Tia Tica catches me and helps rub off the spikes. I scream and holler, of course, but deep down I do appreciate it.

One day Tia Tica was busy getting ready for friends who were coming for lunch. I sat on her shoulder while Tia busied herself with setting the table and fixing the salads. We make a good team, so I just rode around on her shoulder while Tia Tica took care of things.

Just before the friends were expected to arrive, Tia Tica sat down in the living room to rest for a few minutes. Then Tia noticed that I was not on her shoulder.

Nor was I on my cage.

I didn't answer when Tia Tica called me.

Tia Tica began to get quite frantic and started looking everywhere she had been.

Tia Tica looked on the floor and around my cage.

Tia looked on the counter in the bathroom.

She looked near my perch in the dining room.

"Where's Tico?"

Finally Tia Tica looked in the refrigerator.

There I was on the second shelf - where I had stepped off 15 minutes before. It was dark inside because the light goes off when the door is closed.

So I took a nap.

Tia Tica was VERY happy to find me!

Each evening in the summer, Bill, Tia Tica and I go into our screened tree house and wait for the sun to go down. I enjoy sitting on Bill's shoulder while he reads a magazine or looks at things with his binoculars.

Sometimes I'll join Tia Tica while she plays some music or does something on her computer. I like hanging out with them.

When the sun finally goes down, I'm all fluffed up and hunkered down, ready to go to sleep.

You know what?

I think I'm a lucky bird

to have found

Tia Tica and Bill.

LUNATICO CONURE

(aka Tico) is a half moon conure. Conures, in general, are small macaws - parrots with pointed tails and skin, not feathers, around the eyes. Tico has yellow skin around his eyes, orange feathers at the peak of his beak, mostly green feathers on his back and yellow-green feathers on his belly. There are beautiful blue feathers here and there on his wings and head. He thinks he's quite a handsome bird.

His yellow-trimmed eyes are on the sides of his head. That's so he can see if something is sneaking up on him. You cannot see his ears because they are hidden by feathers, but he can hear quite well. He hears a lot of things when no one knows that he's listening. Then later, he will imitate the sound he heard.

You can see two nostrils at the top of his beak, but some people say that conures cannot smell well. It doesn't seem to bother him.

For a parrot Tico is small. He weighs two-and-a-half ounces and is about seven inches long. That's about the size and weight of an Animal Cracker box. Put him on your shoulder, and you'll hardly know he's there.

On each foot Tico has four toes - two pointed forward, two back. When he walks around, his front toes point to one another. Because of that, some people say that he's "pigeon-toed." He's not. He's "conure-toed."

CAROL ATKINSON DURR

(aka Tia Tica) invited Tico into her life in 2002 when grandchildren began arriving - in distant states.

Born and raised in Richmond, Virginia, Carol now lives in Pasadena, Maryland, with her husband, Bill. They own and operate Hammock Island Marina on the western shore of the Chesapeake Bay. She has been designing and creating Christmas cards for the Durr family for over 40 years. Many of her Christmas designs have featured her family life and animals - wild, domestic and imaginary.

For many years she freelanced as a professional calligrapher,
addressing thousands of invitations
and writing the occasional love note.
Although Carol has created many one-of-a-kind books,
Tico's Book is the first to be commercially produced.

For additional copies of *Tico's Book*
contact Carol Durr
8083 Ventnor Road
Pasadena, Maryland 21122
(410) 437-1870
thedurrs@aol.com

Tico's Book was created, illustrated and designed
by Carol Atkinson Durr,
using color pencils,
an iMac OS X,
Photoshop CS 2
&
Quark X Press 7.
The font is Lucida Casual.